Educators Love STEP-UP Books.
So Do Children.*

In this exciting series:

- THE WORDS ARE HARDER (but not too hard)
- THERE'S A LOT MORE TEXT (but it's in bigger print)
- THERE ARE PLENTY OF ILLUSTRATIONS (but they are not just picture books)
- And the subject matter has been carefully chosen to appeal to young readers who want to find out about the world for themselves. These informative and lively books are just the answer.

*"STEP-UP BOOKS

. . . fill a need for precise informational material written in a simple readable form which children can and will enjoy. More please!"—EVELYN L. HEADLEY, *Director of Elementary Education, Edison, New Jersey.*

"I love them."—STEVE MEYER, *second grade pupil, Chicago, Illinois.*

Meet the Men who Sailed the Seas is a book designed to introduce children to the broad sweep of history through the exciting stories of famous men and sailing ships. Included are the voyages of such mariners as Leif Ericson, Christopher Columbus, Francis Drake, and John Paul Jones. It is the story of the men who discovered and shaped the world we live in today.

This title was originally catalogued by the Library of Congress as follows: Dyment, John. Meet the men who sailed the seas. Illustrated by Victor Mays. New York, Random House [1966] 85 p. col. illus. 22 cm. (Step-up books) I. Sea stories— Juvenile literature. I. Mays, Victor, 1927- illus. II. Title.   G570.D9   j910.4   67—643   ISBN: 0-394-80064-8   ISBN: 0-394-90064-2 (lib. bdg.)

Meet the MEN who SAILED the SEAS

By JOHN DYMENT

Illustrated by VICTOR MAYS

Step-Up Books ⌐_⌐ Random House
New York

FOR JUDY

JOHN DYMENT was born in Ottawa, Canada. As a boy he sailed, read Sherlock Holmes, and dreamed of becoming a detective. Instead, he went to McGill University and the Harvard Business School, and now works as a consultant, designing management information systems for businesses. Among other things, he spends his spare time studying history, languages, science, and mathematics, preparing lectures, writing and sailing.

Mr. Dyment, his wife and children live in Larchmont, New York.

VICTOR MAYS wrote and illustrated his first book in 1953 while serving in the Navy. *Fast Iron* was a story about whaling, and it won the Boys' Clubs of America Gold Medal for excellence. Since then he has lent his talented hand to the illustration of many historical books for children, including the three Step-Up Books *Meet George Washington, Meet Christopher Columbus* and *Meet the Men who Sailed the Seas. His first* love has always been the sea, and of all the many themes he has illustrated, seafarers and the ships they sailed in have remained his favorites.

Mr. Mays is a Yale graduate and a commander in the Naval Reserve. He lives in Clinton, Connecticut, with his wife and children.

Contents

1
THE FIRST SAILORS

Men have always looked out to sea and dreamed of what lies beyond. For thousands of years the only way men could cross the sea was in a ship with sails.

No one knows when the first sailing ship was built. One of the oldest pictures of a sailing ship was found on a pot. It was painted in Egypt 5,000 years ago.

But there were ships long before this picture was painted.

The first boat was probably a log. A man could sit on a log and paddle with his hands.

Later, man learned to dig out the inside of a log. Then he could sit in it and paddle.

Then man learned that the wind could move his boat along.

The early sailing ships had to be paddled when the wind did not blow. But when the wind blew, a square sail would be opened. The wind would fill the sail and push the ship through the water.

Most of the oldest pictures of sailing ships come from Egypt. Ships were very important to the Egyptians. Their farms and cities were all along the great river Nile. Egyptian ships moved up and down the Nile. They brought food from the farms to the cities. They carried stone for building great palaces and pyramids. They carried the cloth, oil and gold that were traded between cities. The Nile was a very busy river.

The Nile begins deep in Africa. It flows into a great sea called the Mediterranean. Along the shores of the Mediterranean Sea there were many other countries.

One Mediterranean country near Egypt was Phoenicia. Phoenician sailors were the best of their time. They traded with countries far away from their own land. They built cities on distant shores of the Mediterranean Sea. From these cities, the Phoenicians traded with the people of Africa and Spain.

One of the greatest Phoenician cities was in Africa. This city was called Carthage. Over the years its ships and trade made Carthage very rich. It became one of the most powerful cities in the world.

2
HANNO OF CARTHAGE

About 2,500 years ago a sailor left Carthage on a great voyage. His name was Hanno. Hanno was in command of a large fleet of ships. The ships were crowded with people.

Hanno sailed to the western end of the Mediterranean Sea. There, there are two great rocks. These rocks are called the Pillars of Hercules. Past these rocks is the huge Atlantic Ocean. Hanno and his fleet sailed between the Pillars of Hercules into the Atlantic Ocean.

Hanno turned south. His ships sailed down the coast of Africa. At many places they stopped to leave people. These people were to build cities. From these cities they could trade with African people who lived near by.

Hanno sailed on farther. He wanted to learn about people and places far down the coast.

Hanno and his sailors came to a river. They decided to explore it. They found the river filled with crocodiles. Wild people on shore threw rocks at Hanno's ships.

Farther south they came to an island. At night they heard the sound of drums and strange cries.

Hanno and his men were afraid. But they still sailed on. They came to a place where fire poured down from a mountain. It was a volcano. For four days they sailed past shores covered with flames.

Farther and farther south they sailed. But their food was running low. So they turned about. Then they began the long journey back up the coast of Africa. They sailed through the Pillars of Hercules, and home to Carthage.

Hanno wrote down the story of his voyage. Many people read about the places he had seen. From explorers like Hanno, people learned more and more about far-off lands.

3
THE BATTLE OF SALAMIS

For hundreds of years warships from Carthage guarded the Pillars of Hercules. These warships would let only Phoenician traders sail into the Atlantic.

A ship of war had a ram in front of it. The ram was a piece of wood. It stuck out of the ship's bow near the water. In sea fights warships tried to sink enemy ships by ramming them. Usually the side with the most ships won. This was true until the Battle of Salamis.

At Salamis there was a great sea battle between Greece and Persia.

Greece and Persia were lands across the Mediterranean Sea from Egypt. About the time of Hanno's voyage, Persian armies conquered Egypt and Phoenicia. Xerxes, the king of Persia, wanted to become the ruler of the world.

Xerxes led a great army into Greece. In the sea near by sailed his mighty fleet. Xerxes had more than 700 ships of war.

The leader of the Greeks was a man named Themistocles. He had only 300 warships. But he was a clever man. He set a trap for the Persians.

Themistocles sent his ships into a bay behind the Greek island of Salamis. Then he sent a message to Xerxes. Themistocles pretended that he was a friend of the Persians. He told Xerxes where the Greek ships were. He also said the Greeks would soon sail away.

Xerxes wanted to catch all the Greek ships together. He could then try to sink them all in one big battle.

Xerxes ordered his ships to attack the Greek ships at Salamis. Then he ordered his throne to be put high on a hill overlooking the bay. Xerxes sat on his golden throne and watched the battle below.

Over the sea came Xerxes' mighty fleet. Line after line of Persian ships surged through the water. They filled the narrow mouth of the bay. Then, as Themistocles had planned, the Greeks attacked.

The Greek rams crashed into the Persian ships. Oars were snapped off. Ships were tipped over.

Still more Persian ships crowded into the bay. The ships in back pushed against the ships in front. Oars became tangled. Persian ships rammed into each other. Hundreds of Persian ships were sunk. The rest turned and sailed for home.

Xerxes saw his fleet defeated before his eyes. Themistocles had shown the world that a good battle plan could win a war at sea.

4
PYTHEAS

Greece had long been a land of great traders. Their ships had sailed far down the Mediterranean Sea. In many places they had built cities. One of these was in France. It was called Massilia.

About 100 years after the Battle of Salamis, a man named Pytheas was born in Massilia. He became a famous scientist and sea captain.

One day, some traders came to see Pytheas. They asked him to find the islands that tin came from.

Tin was worth a lot to the traders. It was used in making swords and spears for Greek soldiers. The traders knew the tin came from islands far to the north. It was brought down the rivers of France to Massilia.

Pytheas said he would go. He was a man who wanted to know more about the world. This trip would give him a chance to see the lands and people of the North.

Pytheas probably traveled across France to get to the Atlantic Ocean. He then sailed north. He found an island where people dug tin from the ground. The island was called Britain.

Pytheas lived for a while with the people of Britain. He sailed all around the island and measured each of its sides. Some people in Britain told him of a land farther to the north. Pytheas sailed to this land. He called it Thule.

From the people of Thule he heard that even farther north the sea turned to ice. He was told that there the sun never set in summer.

When Pytheas got back to Massilia, he wrote a book. The book told the story of his trip. It told the people of the Mediterranean many things they had not known before. For the first time they learned that people lived far, far to the north.

5
THE VIKINGS

About the year 800 fierce raiders came over the sea from a land north of Britain. They attacked towns on the coasts of the north countries. These raiders were called Vikings.

The Vikings were armed with axes and swords. They carried away gold and silver, sheep and cows. They even carried away people to be their slaves. Anyone who tried to stop them was killed.

To the north and west of Britain is an island called Iceland. In the year 860 Viking raiders came to Iceland. There were not many people living there. The Vikings killed most of them and took over the land. Then many Vikings moved their families to Iceland. There they hunted and fished and farmed.

In the year 963 a Viking named Eric the Red came to Iceland. He became a leader of many of the Vikings there. He was a bold, fierce man. He often fought with other Vikings. In one fight, Eric killed the sons of a man named Thorgest. Thorgest was liked by many of the Viking leaders.

These leaders held a meeting. They said that Eric must leave Iceland for three years. If he did not leave, he would be killed.

Eric left.

With his family and friends, Eric sailed west. He had heard that to the west there was another island. After sailing for about three days, they found the island. It was the island of Greenland.

Eric lived in Greenland for three years. Then he went back to Iceland. He told people about the land he had visited. He said the hunting and fishing were good. Many Viking families from Iceland followed Eric back to Greenland.

6
THE VIKINGS FIND AMERICA

In the summer of the year 985, a man named Bjarni Herjolfsson set out for Greenland. For three days he and his sailors had good weather. Then the sky grew dark. A storm struck the little ship. The wind blew the ship far to the south and west of Greenland.

After a few days the skies cleared. A day later Bjarni saw land. He knew it was not Greenland. Bjarni sailed north along this strange land for a few days. Then he turned east. Finally, he found Greenland.

Bjarni told Eric the Red about the land to the west. Many years later Eric's son, Leif, sailed with Bjarni back to the new land. Leif probably went there to find wood. In Greenland it was hard to find the right wood for building ships.

Leif named the new land Vinland. He and his men stayed there for the winter. They hunted and fished and cut down trees. In the spring they put the wood on their ship. Then they sailed back to Greenland.

Vikings made many trips to the new land. Some tried to live there. But the Vikings were not the only people in this land. People had been there for thousands of years.

The Vikings called these people Skraelings. There were many fierce fights between the Vikings and the Skraelings. The Vikings often won. But the Skraelings kept attacking them. At last the Vikings left the new land for good. They went back to Greenland. There they could live in peace.

Today we call the Skraelings Indians. And we call their land America.

Over the years Viking stories of this land to the west were forgotten. Traders of the Mediterranean were more interested in stories of lands to the east. The best known stories were told by Marco Polo.

7
MARCO POLO

Marco Polo was born in the Mediterranean city of Venice about 1254. When he was 17, his father and uncle took him on a long, long journey. They went east, to the court of Kublai Khan in China.

Kublai Khan was the emperor of many countries of the East. He liked the Polos. They were clever men. For many years he sent them on trips to watch over his business.

On some of these trips Marco Polo sailed far into eastern seas. He saw cities with palaces. He saw jewels and silks and costly spices.

And he heard stories of Cipango. This was an island near China. Today we call it Japan. Cipango was said to have been the richest land of all. It had jewels and pearls and gold. There was even a palace with a roof covered with gold.

After working 17 years for the Khan, the Polos wanted to return home to Venice. About this time three men from Persia were at the Khan's court. They, too, wanted to travel west. They were taking a beautiful young girl to Persia to marry their king. They asked the Khan to let the Polos guide them. The Khan said yes.

With 14 large ships they set sail.

The voyage to Persia took three years. The Polos left the girl there. Then they traveled on to Venice.

A year later there was a war between Venice and another city. Marco was captured. He spent a year in prison. There he told the story of his adventures to another prisoner. This man wrote down all that Marco told him. Copies of Marco's story were made. They were read by people in many lands.

People were excited by what Marco said about the East. They were most interested in Cipango. For hundreds of years men dreamed of Cipango's gold-roofed palace and the many riches of the East.

8
CHRISTOPHER COLUMBUS

One man who dreamed of the riches of the East was Christopher Columbus. In 1486 he came to see Queen Isabella of Spain. He came to ask her for some ships.

Columbus wanted to sail to the Indies. This was the name given to the lands Marco Polo had told about. The trip had taken Marco three years. Columbus believed he would find the Indies only a month's sail from Spain. He would go a way no one had gone before. He would go west, across the Atlantic Ocean.

Columbus showed the Queen why he thought the Indies were not far across the Atlantic. He showed her maps and letters. They were by men who thought they had figured out how big the world was. These men said that Cipango and China were not far to the west of Spain.

Queen Isabella was not sure. She asked some learned men to decide. Columbus waited for four years. Finally, the learned men told the Queen what they thought.

They said that Columbus was wrong. The world was much bigger around than Columbus thought. There were thousands of miles of ocean between Spain and Cipango.

Ships could not carry enough food for such a long trip.

Columbus did not give up. For two more years he tried to prove he was right. The Queen thought about what Columbus said. If he was right, Spain would become very rich. Spanish traders could bring back the riches of Cipango. If he was wrong, Spain would lose only a few ships. The Queen decided to help Columbus. She would get him his ships.

Soon Columbus had three ships and the men to sail them. In August, 1492, they set out to sea. They headed west, in search of the Indies.

9
ACROSS THE ATLANTIC

Into the unknown sea Columbus' little ships sailed. A good wind carried them steadily to the west.

They sailed for a month. If the maps Columbus had were right, they should have reached Cipango by then. The sailors were frightened. They wanted to turn back.

Columbus told them to sail on. If they did not find land in three more days, he would turn back.

For two more days they sailed west. Very early on the third day, a sailor cried out, "Land. Land!"

Ahead of them was an island. Columbus was sure this island was part of the Indies.

Columbus and some of his men went ashore. On the beach they fell to their knees. They said a prayer of thanks.

Columbus found people living on the island. Because he thought he had reached the Indies, Columbus called the people Indians.

The Indians guided him to other islands near by. But on none of these islands did he find silks or jewels or palaces.

At last he sailed back to Spain.

In Spain Columbus told Queen Isabella he had found the Indies. The Queen sent him across the Atlantic three more times. Each time he hoped to find the riches of the East.

To the day he died, Columbus thought he had reached the Indies. But the Indies were really thousands of miles farther west. Columbus had found something far more important than a short way to the Indies. He had found America.

10
FERDINAND MAGELLAN

After Columbus, many men sailed
across the Atlantic. They soon
learned that Columbus had not
found the Indies. The Indies must
be somewhere beyond the land of
North and South America. But how
were ships to get past this land?

In 1519 five ships crossed the Atlantic from Spain. Their leader was Ferdinand Magellan. Magellan thought that far to the south there might be a way around the new land.

For many months Magellan's ships sailed down the Atlantic coast of South America. Summer passed. Three of Magellan's captains wanted to turn back. They did not think he would ever find a way past South America.

The ships sailed into a bay. There the three captains planned to kill Magellan. Then they would sail back to Spain. They tried to take over the fleet. This was mutiny!

Magellan moved to stop them. At night he sent some men in a small boat. Quietly, they sneaked up on one of the mutineers' ships. They climbed on board. There was a fight. The ship's captain was killed. With that, his men gave up.

Magellan now had three ships. He ordered them to guard the way out of the bay. The mutineers' ships were trapped. They still tried to escape. But they ran into Magellan's ships and were captured.

Magellan punished the captains who had mutinied. He had one captain's head cut off. He left the other to die on shore. Then with his five ships, he sailed on south.

Magellan's troubles did not end. One ship was wrecked on a rock. The rest sailed on. A year had passed since they left Spain. At last they came to a passage between high cliffs. Could this be the way past South America?

11
AROUND THE WORLD

Magellan's four ships sailed into the passage. Icy winds blew over them. They were in great danger of being smashed against the cliffs. They sailed down the passage for five weeks. In a storm Magellan lost sight of his other ships. He sailed on. Suddenly his ship was out of the passage. Ahead of him was a great ocean. He had found the way past America!

Magellan named the ocean the Pacific. Two ships followed him into the Pacific. But there was one ship missing.

There had been another mutiny. The ship had turned back to Spain.

The three ships set out to cross the Pacific. Soon they ran short of food. The biscuits that were left were full of worms. The drinking water was covered with slime. The men were so hungry they ate rats. Many came down with scurvy. This was a terrible sickness that struck sailors on long voyages. Men with scurvy died slowly, in great pain.

Magellan's ships sailed for four months across the Pacific. At last they came to some islands. There they found food and water.

At another group of islands they had a fight with the island people.

Hundreds of warriors attacked them. Magellan was hit by a spear. He fell, and the warriors killed him. His men ran back to their boats.

The ships were leaking badly. One was left behind. Only two ships finally reached the Indies.

The trip home was long and hard. Another ship was lost. Now only one ship, the Victoria, was left. Around Africa and up the Atlantic she sailed. In September, 1522, the Victoria reached Spain.

Magellan had left Spain with five ships and about 270 men. Only 18 men returned on the Victoria. They were the first men to sail all the way around the world.

12
FRANCIS DRAKE

Magellan's trip had shown how big the world really was. The Indies were farther west than anyone had thought. But the Spanish found great riches much closer to home. They discovered the riches of South America.

The Spanish found Indian cities filled with gold and silver. They conquered the Indians. They put Indians to work loading Spanish treasure ships. The ships brought these riches to Spain.

Queen Elizabeth of England did not want Spain to become rich and powerful. Spain and England had been enemies for many years. Queen Elizabeth was afraid Spain would become powerful enough to attack England. She sent sea captains to raid Spanish treasure ships. One of the boldest English captains was Francis Drake.

In 1577 Drake sailed around South America into the Pacific. These were Spanish seas. The Spanish did not think an English ship would dare sail there. Drake surprised them. His ship had more guns than the Spanish treasure ships. He captured many of them.

Drake filled his own ship with the gold, silver and jewels he captured. But he was afraid the Spanish might have sent warships after him. So he decided not to sail back the way he had come. Instead, he sailed west.

Drake sailed across the Pacific, around Africa, and home to England. His ship was the second to sail around the world.

13
THE SPANISH ARMADA

Queen Elizabeth went on board Drake's ship. Drake bowed before his queen. A nobleman touched Drake's shoulder with a sword. The Queen said, "Rise, Sir Francis Drake." She had made him a knight. This was a great honor.

The English went on raiding the Spanish treasure ships. They attacked Spanish towns in America. They also helped the country of the Netherlands in a war with Spain.

King Philip of Spain decided to stop the English. He gathered a great fleet of ships. The fleet was called the Invincible Armada.

In 1588 the Armada set sail. On board were 20,000 soldiers. With this army King Philip planned to conquer England.

The Armada sailed north, toward England. The English sailed out to meet the Spanish. The English had smaller but faster ships. And they were better sailors.

The English ships raced between the huge Spanish ships. The Spanish guns roared. Many of the Spanish shots passed over the heads of the English sailors. The English aimed their guns low. Their shots smashed into the sides of the Spanish ships.

For ten days the two fleets fought. Many Spanish ships burned and sank. Thousands of Spaniards died.

The English were winning. The Spanish ships fled north. They were struck by storms. Some of them were wrecked. Only half the great Armada returned to Spain.

The English had shown that they were the masters of the sea. They had ended forever the danger of Spain's conquering England.

14
THE MAYFLOWER

Many English sea captains had explored the coast of North America. They told people about the new land. Some English people decided to move to America.

In 1620 the ship Mayflower left England. On board were crowded 102 men, women and children. These people were the Pilgrims.

Most of the Pilgrims were afraid. They had never been so far out to sea before. Storms struck the little ship. The Pilgrims were cold and wet. Many of them were sick.

The Mayflower took more than two months to cross the Atlantic. But at last the Pilgrims reached America.

The Pilgrims had different reasons for coming to America. Some came because they were very poor. They could not find work in England. Some came because of their religion. In England they were punished if their religion was different from the king's. They wanted to be able to worship in their own way. Some came looking for adventure in this wild land.

Life in America was very hard. After the first terrible winter only half the Pilgrims were still alive.

But in America the Pilgrims could choose their own leaders. They could make their own laws. When the Mayflower sailed back to England, not one Pilgrim sailed with her.

In time, thousands of families crossed the Atlantic. People settled in different places. The places that they settled were called colonies. Before long there were 13 English colonies in North America.

People in the colonies cleared the land and fought the Indians. They hunted, fished, farmed and traded. Towns and villages grew into cities. The English colonies in America were growing strong.

15
CAPTAIN COOK

Spain had found great riches in South America. England had rich colonies in North America. People in England believed more lands might be found. These lands could be in the Pacific Ocean. Not many ships had explored the Pacific.

In 1767 some of the most famous scientists in England held a meeting. They were members of a club called the Royal Society. Before them stood an officer of the English navy. He was James Cook. The scientists asked Cook to explore the Pacific Ocean.

A few months later, Cook set sail. On board his ship he carried many scientists. He also carried tons of cabbage and onions. A few years before, another Englishman had studied scurvy, the terrible sickness of the sea. He had seen that eating vegetables and fruit seemed to stop scurvy. Cook ordered everyone on his ship to eat the cabbage and onions, and to drink lemon juice. Many men did not like cabbage and onions. Cook said they must eat them or be whipped.

After nine months at sea, Cook reached the Pacific island of Tahiti. In all this time not one man had become sick with scurvy.

Some of the scientists studied the stars. Others drew pictures of plants, birds and insects.

After several months, Cook left Tahiti. He sailed on, south and west. He looked for new lands in the Pacific. He came to the islands of New Zealand and Australia. Cook claimed them for England. Then he sailed home.

In England Cook found he was a famous man. He had shown that scurvy could be stopped by eating vegetables and fruit. His maps of the lands he visited were the best ever drawn. And the scientists had brought back new knowledge of Pacific lands.

Cook spent many more years exploring the Pacific. He became more famous than ever. The king made him a captain in the navy. The men of the Royal Society gave him a very great honor. They asked him to become a member of their club.

On his last visit to the Pacific, Cook sailed north. He tried to sail around the top of North America. But there was too much ice. Cook sailed south again. He found the islands of Hawaii.

Captain Cook loved Hawaii. And at first the Hawaiians loved him. They thought he was a god. They gave him gifts.

But the English stayed and stayed. The Hawaiians were worried. The English were taking too much food.

One night the Hawaiians stole a small boat. Cook went ashore. He planned to capture their chief and trade him for the boat. There was a fight. The Hawaiians rushed at Cook. They stabbed him in the back.

Captain Cook had been one of the world's greatest explorers. All over the world people were sad when they heard he was dead.

16
JOHN PAUL JONES

When Captain Cook first set sail, England was already one of the strongest countries in the world. The English king ruled people in many lands. Some people did not want an English king. In America people wanted to rule themselves. In 1776 war started between the American colonies and England.

One of the American leaders was Benjamin Franklin. He went to see the king· of France.

Franklin asked the king to help the colonies. The king said he would. He sent ships to fight the English. He also gave ships to American captains.

One of these captains was John Paul Jones. The French gave him an old trading ship. He named it the Bonhomme Richard. In it, he set out to raid English ships.

In September, 1779, Jones came upon a fleet of English trading ships. A big warship named the Serapis was guarding them. The Serapis turned toward Jones's ship. As they came close, both ships fired their guns. Two of the old guns on Jones's ship blew up. Many men were killed.

The Serapis fired again. Shots smashed into the Bonhomme Richard. The Americans fired back with the guns they had left.

The two ships came together. The English captain saw that Jones's ship was badly hit. He shouted through the noise of battle. He asked if Jones had given up. John Paul Jones shouted back, "No, I have not yet begun to fight." Then the battle raged on.

The American sailors threw ropes with hooks onto the English ship. They tied the two ships together.

American sailors climbed high on their ship's masts. They fired on the English sailors below.

Then an American threw a small bomb into the English ship. The English gunpowder store blew up. There was a terrific explosion. The English guns were wrecked. The captain of the Serapis gave up.

John Paul Jones's bravery had won the battle. He was the first American hero of the sea.

17
THE CONSTITUTION

The American colonies won the war against England. They became the United States of America.

This new country did not have a navy. The government decided to build some warships. One of the first was finished in 1797. It was named the Constitution.

In 1812 a new war broke out between America and England. The English had many big warships. One captain said that his ship, the Guerriere, was the best England had. He said he could beat any American ship in 15 minutes.

In August, 1812, the Guerriere met the Constitution at sea.

The English ship fired. Her shots fell short. Captain Isaac Hull of the Constitution ordered another sail opened. With a burst of speed, he sailed close to the Guerriere.

Now the Constitution's guns roared. The English ship's stern mast was hit, and fell down.

Hull turned and sailed across the bow of the Guerriere. Shot after shot raked the English ship from bow to stern. The Guerriere's other masts came crashing down.

The Guerriere was now helpless. The English captain gave up. The battle had lasted only 25 minutes.

The new American navy had shown that the best of the English ships could be beaten.

18
THE LAST OF THE SAILING SHIPS

Soon after the Constitution was finished, an American built a new kind of ship. He was Robert Fulton. His ship had a steam engine in it.

Fulton called his steamship the Clermont. Other people called it "Fulton's Folly." They did not think it would work. Men had built steamships before. They had not worked well. Some had blown up.

In August, 1807, the Clermont was ready. Her engine was started. Smoke poured from her stack. On her sides, paddle wheels turned.

The people on board clapped and cheered. People in passing boats waved. Fulton's steamship worked! It moved up the river at five miles an hour.

Fulton built many more steamships. They were better than sailing ships for river work. If the wind was light, ships with sails moved slowly. If there was no wind, they stopped. Steamships did not need the wind to keep them going.

The early steamships still had sails. If the wind was right, the sails could be used. Then the engine could be shut off. This saved money. Steam engines burned up a lot of wood or coal.

In England, steamships were built that could cross the Atlantic Ocean. By 1838 steamships crossed the Atlantic in only 15 days.

There were still some things that sailing ships could do better than steamships. Men used sailing ships to hunt for whales. These whalers might stay at sea for more than two years. Steamships could not carry enough coal to stay out that long.

Sails were also better than steam if great speed was needed. Ships carried tea from China to England. The sooner a ship got to England, the fresher the tea would be. In America and England men built huge sailing ships that were very fast.

These were the clipper ships. They were the biggest, fastest and most beautiful sailing ships ever built. The clippers raced each other across thousands of miles of sea.

In 1848 gold was found in California. The clippers carried men and supplies to the gold fields. They raced all the way around South America to California.

The days of the clipper ships did not last long. The rush for gold in California ended. Bigger and better steamships were built. They could make long voyages as well as sailing ships could. And they could carry more than sailing ships.

Gradually, the sailing ships disappeared. The great age of sail was over.

19
JOSHUA SLOCUM

The great men who sailed ships of war and trade and discovery are gone. But today there are still millions of people who sail. They sail in small boats. And they sail just because they love to.

One small-boat sailor who has become famous is Joshua Slocum. In 1895 Captain Slocum set out from Boston. He was alone in his small sailboat, the Spray.

Slocum sailed across the Atlantic. Near the Pillars of Hercules he met a pirate ship. The pirate started to chase him.

The two boats raced through the water. The pirate was faster than the Spray. He was catching up. The wind began to blow harder. They were in a storm. A sudden blast of wind hit the two boats. With a crash, the pirate's mast came down. But the Spray's mast did not break. Slocum was a better sailor than the pirate. He had taken down his sails just in time. Slocum sailed away, safe at last.

Slocum was afraid there were more pirates in the Mediterranean. He sailed back across the Atlantic.

Captain Slocum sailed south. Now he was following the path of Magellan. He had many adventures.

In South America he fought off Indians. In the Pacific he was almost wrecked by storms. Once, a whale nearly ran into his boat.

After three years Joshua Slocum reached America again. He had done something no one else had done before. He had sailed around the world alone.

Joshua Slocum did not discover great riches or new lands. He did not win battles. But he did love the sea, and he had faced its challenge. Hanno, Columbus, Magellan and Cook were men like this. Their spirit of adventure lives on in all who set out to sea with only the wind to carry them.

The
STEP-UP Books

NATURE LIBRARY

ANIMALS DO THE STRANGEST THINGS

BIRDS DO THE STRANGEST THINGS

FISH DO THE STRANGEST THINGS

INSECTS DO THE STRANGEST THINGS

Story of AMERICA

Meet THE NORTH AMERICAN INDIANS   THE ADVENTURES OF LEWIS AND CLARK

Meet THE MEN WHO SAILED THE SEAS   Meet ANDREW JACKSON

Meet CHRISTOPHER COLUMBUS   Meet ABRAHAM LINCOLN

Meet THE PILGRIM FATHERS   Meet ROBERT E. LEE

Meet BENJAMIN FRANKLIN   Meet THEODORE ROOSEVELT

Meet GEORGE WASHINGTON   Meet JOHN F. KENNEDY

Meet THOMAS JEFFERSON   THE STORY OF FLIGHT

A map of
THE WORLD
showing the
Places Talked About
in this Book
and some
Famous Voyages of Discovery